Matinee Light

Matinee Light

Diana Hartog

The Coach House Press, Toronto

Published with the assistance of the Canada Council
and the Ontario Arts Council.

ISBN 0 88910 256 2

For my daughter Selena
and for Jack

One only dies for the first man. COLETTE

Contents

The Common Man

Spring, and all day today in town I noticed
pregnant women — waxing at different stages
but always that same round belly floating by, like a mote
just beyond focus, something I meant to say

— about last night: the presence that eclipsed us both,
that moved out of sight if we looked — what was it we held
as we held each other? When it left
it left me your face: luminous, blinded

and I remembered how you put down your fork in the restaurant
and leaning over, murmured in my ear 'I love you for saying
"I hate you fo saying that"'
— from our public argument about the common man
when you'd spat out 'Well it ain't Rilke!' —

your mouth sad from the side, the way it looked
the night we met, the curve of your forehead
rising above the horizon, legions of deer
leaping to the right across your chest
— I love that sweater, you never wear it anymore.

A Thousand Thousand Leaves

Every coiled green leaf
on every birch in the valley
opens today
and the lake is still
and all day long I'll stop and remember.

All day long the heart's
dark bud unfurls
coils for its quick season
— How could I forget
you, Heart?

April 27, 79

A Critical Piece

The parachute is tangled and I'm drifting off course.
I've been sent to retrieve a critical piece, but as far
as I can see there's nothing left. I've landed, the ground
is still warm, my typewriter's fine. A child slouching
in a doorway confesses to accepting candy from a stranger
after I slip her my last mint. I ignore the toothless man
collapsed on the sidewalk; he waves his cane at my ankles,
claims his gold fillings have been stolen. I'm talking to
an eye-witness, a waitress in the cafe: 'Yes, you used to sit
at that table in the corner — Don't you remember that
piece you wrote about me?' It's a fact: her Irish face
is gone, and that obscene way she had of gripping her pencil.
I make discreet inquiries about a boyfriend, thinking this
will lead to a long courtship and then the ring she's hiding in
the pocket of her skirt — perhaps on her left hand, perhaps on
her third finger: an opal similar if not identical to the one
I'll inherit from Mother.

I Drew a Hair

I drew a hair from my sandwich
and held it to the light: his or mine?

His eyes are near the blue
of one of your pale skies — August, say.

I laid my ear to the moss of his chest and imagined
your great heart, booming beneath fields.

Poem Found on Freeway!!

Housewife weighing 98 lbs. lifts crumpled fender
of 2 ½ ton truck while staring down into ardent eyes
of victim — old high school boyfriend who dropped
her

Widower sitting on toilet proposes after surviving
skidding tires splintered living room splintered
hall splintered bathroom door when semi driven by widow
stops inches short of his knees

Infant placed on vw roof and
forgotten as distracted parents drive off down freeway
found safe face down in ditch observing ants
and babbling Whitman's 'I Sing the Body Electric'

Poet working nights for steel-town newspaper
accused of planting bizarre miraculous events as God's truth
seen forced into police car and driven off
into fiery dawn of creation

Evening

The sun is rose, heavy on its stem,
having waited all day for this:
the two of us rocking on the porch
admiring it like a flower in our garden.

A Hole

I know everything about digging a hole and then
the sides begin to dribble back down into its
perfect emptiness — not from the dark clay carved
by the tip of my shovel but above that, small stones
dropping from exposed roots, or higher still, tiny
sharp ones, pouring from a loosened pocket of shale
like a sudden remembrance, the lip crumbling under my
boot as the dirt dries, dirt that sifts down the sides
as I scoop it with my hands, dirt as large as a boulder
but feathery, with no edges, something I was going to
say.

Black Tulips
for Paul Dutton

He plants his feet apart and eyes calm
curls forward,
unfurls as a wail blossoms from his mouth – frays.

He sucks a breath, bends again as if in pain
and a fresh cry spines up perpendicular to my thought
'Is this real or the blues?'
and splays open in the air: dark, quivering.

He is gathering these for us, gathering a fistful.

Card Game

Dark
warm under my dome of coats
wool and fur

the murmur from the kitchen
catching fire
the spark of my mother's laugh

and me in here a beaver
hot
hid from Mr. Girardi's breath

me in here playing dead
dreading 'Where's my girl?'
and the bed quivering under his knee.

On the Ferry

There's a look about a girl of twelve or so,
a swell of tides testing channels,
the smell of sea and sea-weeds, waters
tentative, tenacious, pressing out the flesh.

Rocking as the boat rocks, she circles the deck,
she makes a dance of it — hiding in her hair as she passes.
What has she to do with a stranger's stare
'How could you have been a girl?'

What can I tell her? — lifted as she is to this shape
without a say, without a choice except to be it: sea-stuff.
It seemed a lesson for another species, when I resisted
all that flowing through me.

Angel Island, March 73

On the Occasion of a Death by Suicide

A delicate subject, followed in academic journals:
some propose the mind hovers above the brain,
others, Materialists, have it   kit & kaboodle.

Some, past theory, merely aim up
through the mouth.
Fact/pain — we all know the general direction.

A neighbor, one who assumes odd jobs, cleaned up the mess.
I imagine him standing on a chair, stretched,
picking the shards of skull from the ceiling.

I can follow him this far: the evidence
each piece by itself. Right at the last
second my thoughts scatter.

Matilda's Dress

Stretched naked on the rumpled spread
he fists the pillows — waves of carefully
hand-embroidered roses lapping against his skin, against
the length of him.

Beyond the window, on a line strung between two grey trunks
I notice a dress — black, hung alone,
pinned by one limp flung-over sleeve
and a fan of skirt, caught to one side in a curtsy.

'My aunt,' he says in English from the bed. ' — Matilda.
She is forty, never married.
She cares for my mother — there is no story.'

Her dress swells in the rising wind: from here it looks dry.

San Blas 72

All My Senses

I.

I held your face in my hands
and then I held your face in my hands.
Your beard is greyer than I remember, your eyes still
distant blue. The smell of you, your body
pressed against my memory of it — like that, yes.

II.

I'll need a vase.
The black one upstairs
on the shelf
over by the chest. Be careful — there's old
water in it.

III.

That muffled sound behind you: our gorilla
boarded up within the wall — how we wrestled with that one!
both dreaming at the same time.
Remember its smeared features, how it twisted in our grasp?
Here — taste.

Chopin's Moons

One arrowroot cookie remained, scalloped between them on the blue & white china plate set out for tea. It was Sand who spoke first, curious about Chopin's perfectly formed nails and his perfect white moons in descending order from thumb to little finger. 'These are my hands,' he said, regarding their pale arrowroot color, ' — a tiny brain pulsing under each transplanted moon and each dedicated to a different phase of my childhood. Composers, long dead, will often exhaust themselves trying to find room, wedging between my fingers as I play.' Weak, he asked if he might lie down but Sand insisted, propping him on the bench — where he slumped and abandoned his fingers to the keys. Then she crawled underneath and pumped his tiny slippered feet up and down — Ah that sound!: D.H. Lawrence, writing *Piano,* crawled under too, and pumping Sand's cold hands with his own, wept to hear his mother play Chopin so long ago.

The Toaster Salesman

It's chrome gleams, the slice of whole wheat
sinks out of sight as the man adjusts
light to dark and the elements

hum and glow

and I'm left with a bed full of crumbs
and cords snaking off, straining towards outlets —
my hair standing on end.

The Buick

There's some business of a girl wanting a ride in the Buick. He fishes for the keys in the pocket of his white shorts and arcs them jangling and silver through the air and into her hands. The tennis court begins to buckle and heave again and he barely returns the ball. By the end of the set his shirt is damp and he pulls it off over his head, caught for a moment in the folds of his own smell. The long net swells with wind. Eucalyptus leaves skitter across the parking lot. The Buick is back. And dusty, he sees, the radio left on by mistake — 'Apple Blossom Time' pierced with static. On the front seat a purse lies wedged in the crack of the grey flannel upholstery. Its clasp has come open, its lips parted just enough on a little cave, a jumble of my mother's things. All he remembers is thick auburn hair brushing her blouse oh and the backs of her knees, so vulnerable and familiar that again they'd slipped behind his thoughts unnoticed. He rings the doorbell and quick slicks a hand over his head. Waits under the glare of the porchlight in a little circle of 1939.

Nabokov's Lap

A nondescript dog trots up the hill past the dump,
past a clump of ravens curious
about the tongue that dangles from his mouth
but the dog demurs, veers down a long driveway, the author's car
purring at his side.

A narrative, the author thinks, setting the brake
and reaching for his samples. His favorite
slips between the seats
and he pries it out,
dusting his fingerprints from her skin —

the girl rocking naked in her special chair
carved to the shape of Nabokov's lap. She squeezes its
muscled walnut arms — 'Tell me a story!' —
but helpless with love the chair can do nothing more
than stare at the nape of her neck

and the author appears, dazed,
the dog like a briefcase at the end of his arm
— Should he have come?
'One little two little three little Indians' — kneeling
he nibbles her toes.

'That tickles!' The girl squirms in the hapless chair
and small cries are heard
as of a bird caught under a tea-cozy
— the dog leaping to the window,
his pale blue eyes still pitted with ravens —

'... ten little Indian boys!' The author
swallows bits of lint.
'Now dry them,' she demands, wiggling her toes
and the author blows his gentle breath back and forth,
each small nail a fresh photograph.

Isadora Duncan

Ferns bend, fling back their fronds   Wind!

The mountains pretend they are horses
and roll on their backs   Thunder!

The forest pales with turned-up bellies   Rain!

Lightning!
No crickets!

Fighting Dirty

Pondering the equality of the sexes
I sink to my chin and the water level
rises above your bathtub ring a good
four inches.

The Third Muse

bluffs her way into the basement apartment on Whitman's trumpet line,
rifles manuscripts, listens for herself in the room.

The Muse has come specifically to this address and is not disappointed:
Shakespeare's 18th sonnet drones from a tape, recorded by the author

— who lies prone on the orange shag rug, his forehead
battered with red peonies.

The Muse pries at his heart, spills it out like a drawer
and pants in the emptiness. Looks around. Hears that monotone.

She shivers at 'rough winds' and begins to weep, beats this man with her braids
and confesses her ugliness, her running sores — spitting as she rants.

The poet is ecstatic, having dreamt of this visit for weeks.
He takes Erato's face, dribbling and wild, between his hands

and kisses her gently as if she were a runaway teenager.

You Never Did

You never did leave for Japan on that tiny raft
we talked about. I never had the chance
to pack you a lunch or imagine you
bobbing out on the Pacific — our love purer
each day spent apart.

Fate wanted that voyage! She'd made plans, she had in mind
storms of an advanced spiritual nature,
she wanted you tossed on a black poisonous sea
while I on shore would post letters of absolute felicity
— white-winged singing letters
flying low and at a steady pace behind you.

Afternoon at the Movies

TAKE HEART

A bluejay is thicker-skinned and carries more weight than a heart:
let's stuff one in live — scrap what's there now
and stuff in a jay, feathers and all, still beating. Wanting
out as usual.

IN PARIS

There's a bird so small and delicate when roasted
that the man dining alone in the four-star restaurant
places a large white napkin over his head
for the full effect — the tiny crunch like a single perfect thought.
Imagine a dining room filled with people in their white hoods,
blind to the waiters' smiles.

IMPERIALIST DOG

We can still feel it past the feathers:
the tiny throbbing heart of the jay. A pea under the mattress.
The idea remains: replace it with a cockroach, *its* heart
hollowed out for a gnat, the gnat's speck of a heart being
the final Chinese box — the cliché of the final Chinese box
stuffed down its throat.

SILK DRAWERS

Far off, out on the end of the gnat's tongue, we come to a decision:
we see green. A picnic on a suburban lawn.
Impeccable in white, Mind and Heart dine upon each other,
complementing each other's taste
and passing tidbits back and forth — small sacrifice
for what the Heart has in mind.

The Exception

At the screen door he seems nice enough. His face is oddly familiar. I tell him I never do this, this is the exception. He wants to make a phone call but takes over the kitchen instead, starts cooking mushroom soup in an aluminum pan. I explain about aluminum salts. The line is busy, and he lights the fire. I tend it like a small toothache and begin to talk and my tongue starts peeling off in little flames and falling into the fire. 'Don't do that,' he says. The phone rings. It's for him. She is calling from a distant city where she has gone to buy material for the couch. Does he want flowers? I decide to wait out in the garden. I lie on a bench and look up at the map of the stars. It's cold. Through the lighted window I can see him still talking. He paces the room. There's a large worm in his hands and he holds it out from his body: it's writhing and appears to be inconsolable.

Girls, Eleven and Ten

Tonight one wanted to weep
and then the other came up too:
we lay naked on the bed, the three of us
and compared legs — their small thin ones
waving in the air next to mine
and we 'braided' them in a tangle.

— Days, and the house is filled with importance,
their breasts like something we planted.

They are little barques beside me:
I tickle their backs
and trace circles as I sing and we travel.

The Same Spring

This morning as I started out at a fast walk
and felt the sun through the back of my blouse
and smelled the Balm of Gilead
from the firs lining the road,
three men gathering leaves on the golf course
stopped to watch me pass, leaning on their rakes,
and it occurred to me:

This is the same spring Shakespeare wrote about.

Postcard

This isn't much, only 4½ by 5½'s worth.
Think of it as a plot of dry grass,
two inches high and waving. Pretend
it's your roommate's scalp and you're
a gibbon: what's down here among the
roots incites saliva to drool in man or
beast, watering our most perverse desires.
Don't be surprised if your hairline ad-
vances overnight.

Lament

O to write a long poem,
to trail,
to drag a stick along a fence
dut dut dut dut

I Was Reading Yeats

I was reading Yeats when Poe's raven
flew overhead and cawed
and I put my hand up over the sun
and saw blue sky with poplar fluff blowing
as the raven wheeled again.

I heard the wind over its wings — not a pumping sound
but the smooth hiss of a glide, I was that close.
It spiralled up — its wings out stiff, only curving to be lifted
higher around Yeat's tower until a mere
black speck, scribbling: the nib of Poe's pen.

Untitled Sculpture

You handle rain beautifully.
Your shape reminds me of flesh, an organ
pressured into odd angles,

the poem too filling the odd shape of the moment,
entering every fizzure and hole without hesitation,
with the curiosity of water.

A heart then — black, huge with disuse
and that bizarre swelling that happens
when a familiar word is repeated over and over: Heart

flooding into the fingers of my father's hand
as if blowing a balloon
and I hold it like his real hand:
as if it would last forever.

Jesse

He looms above her along the bone of a log,
his head already free, his tiny naked body
still wedged between the mountains across the lake.
His mother frowns from where she suns on the sand
as nearing he begins to ascend. She calls him — 'Jesse!' —
but he pretends that's not his name
and smiles down — his blue eyes
weeping of their own accord.

World

Air wanders in, mild and unworried
and strays out again,
the sweet breath of the world;

lolls on the grassy bank among the children
waiting to be born
and the animals, polite, wishing to speak.

Sleep

Through the night
we turn to a rhythm of fold and fit,
testing the line our bodies meet along,
the difference between holding
and being held.

Familiar Ground

Still soaring through the air
I had to run the landscape backwards like a film
to find my body — there! where I left it —

and I woke to rain,
though my dream had been of flying over desert,
the sagebrush far below bent and tortured with thirst.

But it rains, and John phones to say his dog Otto
died in his sleep and is already buried.
Black, bear-like Otto — waking into his body under the orchard.

June 1, 80

You Know What Turns Me On?

When I begin to undress without thinking
and you watch from the bed
and I slip off my blouse and hear a little
oh god.

The Apprentice

On my last visit home I watched from the kitchen window: my
father — out in the back patio on his knees. He'd
take a brick in one hand, weigh it in his open palm
and butter it thick in two deft strokes — here there's a
little jump to seeing it set in. He'd tap the brick into place
with the handle of the trowel, its tip tonguing along the joint,
the pleasure of his own movements like a light around him as
stooped he shadowed his work — nothing beyond his reach and the
slap of mortar. He made it look easy.

Don't talk like that. Death
will hear for sure.
He'll mistake this soft babbling of yours
for words said at the last minute,
it's the love in your voice that he'll smell,
daughter. Haven't I taught you anything?

Produit du Canadodo

Includes
my bare feet, the spots of Rust stain on my bare feet, my grandfather
alseep on the lawn in California, his dream, his feet like mine,
includes this poem, in the best of Post-modern traditions,

Includes Rosalind Russell's intelligent advice on How To Lose A Man,
Katherine Hepburn's notorious discipline, the way the CBC
conspires to separate my day into compartments, the way
I go along,

Includes letters that read like old Cole Porter songs,
bundles of cookies that come untied at the post office,
the combination of Fate/small boats/flat seas, includes giants
with their superior sense of proportion,

Includes anything that is slightly off-key off-color
off-the-wall too short too fat trite, includes my mother's
network of freckles, her ineptness when it comes to
interior decorating or coordinating an outfit,

Includes plants that fail to thrive under the best of
soil conditions, includes bad movies and good popcorn,
the persistence of village idiots into the twentieth century,
a virgin thought loosening its bonds,

Includes the stillness of trees sometimes and that they might
comprehend what we're saying, includes fights, irrevocable words
and the way the room shifts, includes the little beansprout in my
heart when I see a pregnant woman naked at the beach,

Includes its small leap when I turn around in the bank and you've
been standing there watching me, includes the way love
always manages to steer the conversation around to itself, nudging
between every other line like a small water-animal,

Includes the possibility that DNA is short for Love twisting up
and that we're at best helpless, the mind holding on for dear life,
includes Heart as it stands for that small robin beating at the
cage of my hand, as it stands for tight fist,

Includes the illusion of Infinite Grace, includes all the times
I've seen Ginger Rogers and Fred Astaire dancing down the staircase,
includes her taffeta skirt, his white spats, their smiles,
their tiny mistakes.

I'm Right Behind You

You Orpheus? You forget

Artemis follows: that hiss you hear
is not the sea, it's not Eurydice's
quivering voice piercing your heart

It's my arrow.

The People Inside

AIR

I had to kick it off last night – too sticky.
Usually there's never enough, never that satisfaction
of a lungful you read about.

FOOD

The closet eater, the eater of Hide-a-beds, the devoured:
there's a man sitting next to me at the counter
who's eating as if he were hungry and it was natural.

WATER

One takes to drinking whatever's at hand,
whatever tastes thirsty and bottomless, whatever flows
the way I'm going.

SHELTER

Home I guess. One with the solid roof you get when you press
forefingers together, and littlefingers together. The kind
you crack open with your hands to wiggle the people inside.

The Man Who Loved Ordinary Objects

His watch, spent matches, coins, a wadded-up handkerchief —
he digs for these every night in the pockets of his pants
and lays the items out with the care of an archeologist: Who lived
and carried these around?

Dogs bark at him as he gropes for the mail.
The landlady upstairs sweeps her steps and motes of dust
settle on his pale hair, his stooped shoulders.
— He ignores these caresses, leaves events untouched
the way he was taught to resist fledglings fallen from nests

though he saves arguments, cupping them on his palm
the way someone else might display a rare butterfly — Oh
it had hurt: his moan of despair
and how she went to him, dropping her cruelty
like a basket of clothes.

On the Nature of Independence
and the Hypothesis of Free Will

I like to think we're God's slippers:
every time we decide to make love
He's already slipped his feet into the two of us.

Like Famous Japanese Lovers,
We're Thousands of Miles Apart

Forgive this note. Our plan is killing me.
— How can I bear not to phone or even write?
I go dazed around the house. Excuses
pour from me like filth.
My pipe goes out a lot.

Tell me, what's more important —
that I get to work like I'm supposed to,
or should I just lie here on the warm stones,
go over what you said,
feel blessed?

I see you bending, cursing the tulips,
digging too short for their roots — your fingers on fire.

I couldn't tell you over the phone
but I dreamt that you and she were distant twin planets.
To see each face, I had to flounder across —
I'd just reach her
and the vision of your face would come clear
and I'd struggle back, filled with longing.
Again, near, her face would pass in front of yours
like a cloud, and I was sure: it was she I really loved.

My words fly up, meet yours half-way —
over Saskatchewan probably.
The mailbox is dark inside
with a tight slit that snaps shut over my letters
— oh my body wants to come too.

※ ※ ※

I washed your handkerchief and hung it out with my laundry.
— You'd left it knotted up at the bottom of my bed.
It looks nice on the line — pinned between my red blouse
and that slip you like.

The Human Ear

I tried to follow its intricacies on in but the tongue
in my mind jammed as in an earlier attempt to penetrate
all at once the rooms of Schönbrunn Palace, each with its
glorious gold ceiling and enamelled stove.

No wonder we crave cross-sections: what he wants,
what she's thinking, cleaved and opening out,
a Victorian dollhouse, the vaulted chambers stiff with detail —

Ah the heart. That it remains in camera
like a stubborn judge, all that going on
and nothing written down — the lover
a reporter pacing the hall, wild for what he's missing.

Matinee Light   *a movie review*

Bellows, squeals, howls: a cacophony of mating calls
rising from the planet as ants, elephants, ostriches – everything else
except us – did it.

I like the slugs the best, the two flexing like muscles
oh and the swans, they didn't make a wrong move: the football star
and his date on prom night – gliding across the gym.

They stuffed in death as filler, a pair of spent salmon
draped from a low-hanging branch, their shredded flesh
trailing in the water, their spines elegantly bent musical instruments.

I winced and thought of you as a lady
praying mantis began to munch her suitor's head: the horror
of his body carrying on like that, pulsing, faithful to her still

as we shuffled out: the couple ahead of me
holding hands – meeting matinee light
with that dazed expression of lovers.

Woodpile

Every day the woodpile
slants in farther.
On the way to the line my arms are always full.
On the way back, it doesn't look *that* bad.

— I suppose I should straighten it,
or I could wait for it, and hearing a sudden
tumble & roar at tea or through sleep I would say
Ah   that must be the woodpile.

Tuolumne River

My mother ankle-deep, wincing at the cold,
tucking all that red hair beneath her cap.
Tilting her head. Looking like that. Again
I tread water, again she wades in — this matter of swimming
something to be done.

I watch
   her white cap
    then her face, laid on the water,
   her blank white cap
   then her face

and I dive — through the glared surface of memory
into cool green water. In the veiled light
I can see the blurred strawberries on her suit like mine
and the fixed triangle her legs form as she stands
waist-deep now, braced against the current.

The river pulls me,
threads me between her knees — past the freckled skin
with its fine hair up close that billows like grass.
I turn, work my way
upstream again: just one last time.

The Size of the Girl

A darkroom blemish burns in the photo like a tiny black sun
above a field where I stand planted, age three, my fists
perfectly equal, gripping a short length of stick
from which a string lifts taut, drawn to the upper
right-hand corner of the sky — to a point out of sight:
a speck of kite I strain to imagine.

The snapshot, propped on my desk, is being approached
by an insect the size of the girl.

Sunny Jim

I sent away for it: a delicate
airplane model from a kit, the pilot
flying with guns blazing and other planes
shooting it out. On the box things look
thick with machinery and footholds

— pieced together, an intricate maze:
bones like matchsticks
scraps of tissue that dry taut —

It's the pilot without his cap!
Under the chinstrap and goggles
the face of a young blue-eyed boy: Sunny Jim
from the label on the peanut butter jar
This is not what I ordered!

Who

If I could stop telling you what's wrong
so you could make it right or untrue

If I could look straight at you without hate
or hope

If I could see us plain and say
Enough!

Who would pick the fluff from your bellybutton?

After Einstein

Apples out of nowhere, apples that happened to be
in the neighborhood
falling all over themselves in a red beaded curtain.

The curtain parts:
we see a woman's buttocks, the long curve of her back
behind a waterfall of apples, liquid

over the beauty of her breasts,
clinging to her stomach, her thighs: this blush
she takes for granted — Eve

naked under the tree,
bending for the bruised ones.

Tonight I Will Dream of a Horse

knee-deep in the current:
he is testing his footing among the stones.

I open the window for air.

He will not look at me
but stares off across the river. Shakes his mane.

I undress. I lie down. I wrap my arms
around his great muscled neck

and ease beneath the waters.

Passing the Buddha on the Way Up

The mist enrobed limbs, boulders, spread
slowly up, snagged by our open mouths

and we portered it down again, losing some as we laughed, passing
that arbutus we passed on the way up, its red arms lifted above the path

as we zigzagged down, plaiting the muddy strand between us
and guessing at the names for plants we

startled on the way up, when we dared not speak but instead
pointed, out breath separate clouds that rose into fog

and we portered it down again, losing some as we laughed
at the thought that silence is more suitable for a mountain.

Any Absence Longer Than a Year

When approaching, each man will lift up a string of fish
overlapping like scales, until the woman in each case
weeps at the sight: here is a man covered in silver.

Or let Love's soldier leave the fish to swim
and instead strip naked, rub himself with leaves
and petals of the flowers that grow outside his woman's tent:
this is *her* smell, it must perfume him like a thought
of her own — as if she had dreamt him and dreams him now.

Let him gather the small bones scattered in the yard — the record
of days she has waited: in grief she spent these, cast them out.
She will see him squatting in the dirt, fashioning her a bracelet.

for C.
July 9, 80

Cherries

Lips purpled with juice
you dip out from under the tree like a guilty summer,
your gift a handful of cherries
but it's your mouth I want.

The Axis is an Imaginary Line

We agree: we're opposites
but then who
leaned back first
and started circling like this
for fun, for some sad reason
as your eyes blur
your mouth grows softly bruised
and you say it's mine
and we always do this — lose
whose fault it is.

The Wisdom of Nature

While you slept, ate, studied, drank too much
your beard grew.
You knew it was growing: the hiss
filtered into your dreams in the disguise
of tires passing on the wet street,

bursts of growth
tearing chunks of flesh like pavement,
the cells
ravaging each other,

hair
springing from underground — hair like a fountain
splitting the boards of the floor
and arcing up through your feet as you typed
without a thought of me. What did you expect?

On the Mathematical Probability
of a Head-on Collision

Here I am heading east thinking of
you heading west and you're probably thinking
mild sexual thoughts as you cruise along, while I'm
passing a lot, vibrating at the perfect frequency
and remembering how love is often best
when you just pull over
and I'll bet you've just speeded up.

Or Do I Have It Backwards?

Somewhere in the closet
there must be a stack of lace-paper doilies left over
from last Valentine's skirmish at the chain-link fence surrounding
that great romantic, the Heart — like King Kong

doomed to escape: we watch the scented white handkerchief drift down
to where the huge beast hunkers, deep in the hold of the ship
— his savage face lifting. We sniff, sniff the air: Spring
lurks in the next crocus.

Even as you read this, you're at risk, for the printed word we're told
heads straight for the left brain
which is on the right side and busy criticizing the technique
of the cameraman while the right brain, which is all wrong

grows moist as Donald Sutherland bends to kiss Jane Fonda in *Klute*
when she has that fever and is finally vulnerable. Never mind
the details, it's that damp clinch: Head wrestling Heart
— oh don't draw the blinds!

I think I'll phone him. Maybe I can get the number
from that friend of his with the handsomely ravaged face,
the one we met by chance that rainy night at a highway phone booth
dialing his mistress who didn't answer.

Madame Love

Someday we'll be relaxed.
It will be like having a cherished guest in the house,
someone sometimes cranky
but with big soft bosoms covered in flowered material
and with a big yellow brooch between them to finger
— What's wrong is the way we treat old people!

Love is a poor relative who has no choice —
may she die of old age, with us on her lap.

Love Poem

You come to me as waters flood,
without knock, beyond keys,
too late to save
what seems important at the time.

Scattered poems, nightgowns,
open, underlined books — all
ravished by your mere presence;
the lick of rug beneath my feet,
even my blue china cups
neat on their hooks — betrayed.

My knees notice first
and then my thighs go;
Dürer's wing, luminous in its frame,
blurs. Nothing matters.

Your lips fade the flowers on the wall:
one by one fall the numbed roses.

Ode to Ontario

– So that I might praise a man newly weaned
from your bright smog, Ontario, one who burns
with the intensity of five steel mills
and has never given in to sanity or beauty,
but one who was constant in recording the geography
of your faults without drawing conclusions. This feat,
to love originally, requires of the brain
benign bruise spots and of the heart
a willingness to observe teeth-marks in the face of love

His face – with its parted hair and choir boy
smile above a perfectly-tied tie and with the basset hound
of Niagara falling all over his lap. Androgynous Ontario,
don't weep. You have lost an amorous poet
but everything to be said for British Columbia
is easily said – a lush whorl of fir compared
to your flat belly and the modest mound
of Mount Hope. Remember, he is almost forty
and you have been everything to him – chum,
lover, hag. He could see into your future
and saw himself there, beating you with a cane,
blaming you for your distance. Yes –

I have taken him in my arms, folded him within
new species of vegetation and mountains
he will never learn the names of.
He will never know me as he has known you, Ontario:
heading west towards the East, he wants secrets now
and throws himself on the ridge of my body
in vain, in successive waves of consciousness.

A Glimpse of Heaven

A blank white sheet creates whatever it covers
the way a perfect whitesauce reveals
the deserving poem, rendering it visible and intimating
certain interesting practices going on underneath,

Snow falling, caressing the small poem at the stoplight,
a poem obedient to the arbitrary authority of interruptions
but quietly alert, its little motor
idling under a light hand,

Turning over in my mind
like the symbolic worm in a bottle of Mescal —
conscious of its fate and its duty to contribute
to the idea of the hero —

While all that separates me from my return is the body of the poem
lolling languid and flesh-colored under the sheet,
faithful to my memory but blessed with a healthy approach to change
— greeting each new line with a glimpse of heaven.

Some of these poems appeared previously in *CROSS-COUNTRY,
Capilano Review, B.C. Monthly, Island, Malahat Review, Rolling
Stone* and *Waves.*

My thanks to Eveline Van Ginkel for editorial assistance
and continuing support.

Edited for the press by bpNichol.
Cover design by Gordon Robertson.
Typeset in Stempel Garamond and printed in Canada.

For a list of other books you might enjoy,
write for our catalogue of books in print,
or call us at (416) 979-2217.

The Coach House Press
401 (rear) Huron Street
Toronto, Ontario
M5G 2G5